MW00528921

CRITICAL THINKING

A Practical Guide to
Solving Problems and
Making the Right Decisions
at Work and in Everyday Life.

Think Critically,
Develop Effective Communication,
Improve Your Listening Skills

MORRIS CULLEN

4

Table of Contents

Introduction

Strong critical thinkers are more effective in life. They can approach situations in ways that make more sense and can be defended logically. They are less prone to being caught into behaving in ways that are impulsive or incorrect, and because of that, you must learn to be a critical thinker. The critical thinker is going to find that getting through life is simply easier – it is everywhere in life. In so many situations around you, the ability to think critically is necessary, from how likely you are to succeed in a job that is quite technical and mathematical to how likely you are to have a happy and successful relationship.

How to Work on Critical Thinking

We try to develop communication and critical thinking skills through conversation in its possible forms:

- The dialogue, which we will define as a cooperative and two-way conversation. The objective is for participants to exchange information and establish relationships among themselves. In favorable conditions, it can be the best tool to develop critical thinking, creativity, learning.

- Discourse is a one-way cooperative conversation. The aim is to deliver relevant information from the speaker to the listeners.

- Diatribe is a competitive, one-way conversation. The goal is to express emotions, intimidate those who disagree with us, and/or inspire those who share the same perspective.

We gather ideas in very different formats (questions, moral dilemmas, provocative statements, stories, jokes, social experiments, words) to set up targeted conversations with project participants.

Always remember that critical thinking is a nonstop process. If you discover new information that shows situations in a different light, examine this new information and decide whether it changes, or shapes your opinion on a subject.

Chapter 1.
Critical Thinking in the Professional World

Everywhere you go, and with anything you do, critical thinking is a skill that is extremely necessary for all aspects of the workforce. It allows employers and employees to look at a situation from all angles and weigh every solution possible before coming up with a direct answer.

Creates Options: Not only does critical thinking encourage people to work together and come up with new ideas, but it allows people to come up with multiple solutions to one problem. The situation may require more than one solution that an individual may not have thought of otherwise, or it may only require one solution. Still, the company has several options that they can now use to solve the problem. It also allows for the chance to use resources that are already available instead of having to spend money on new things. Additionally, it gives customers options, as well.

Uncovers Spinoffs: While the group can come up with options for one solution, critical thinking allows for completely new ideas to come out of those solutions. You and your co-workers may be talking about one thing, and suddenly someone comes up with how that option can be applied to a completely different aspect of the company.

Once you start asking questions and coming up with ideas, you can address other unsolved topics.

While critical thinking can be generally applied to all professions at different levels, there are some professions where critical thinking is imperative to the success of not only the worker and the company, but the choices made through critical thinking have a major impact on the people they are involved with. In these professions, if the thinking is not critical and not supported by truth arguments, the consequences of that can be fatal or very dangerous.

Focus on Resilience

A key characteristic of the critical thinker is to remain resilient in the face of adversity. This is an overall important life skill to have because when you find yourself blocked by any kind of obstacle, you can push through it and keep achieving. With a sense of resiliency, you understand that what worked before will not always work in the future. You know that you have to have more options and a broader palette.

Be Honest About Your Biases

There are a few ways to counteract bias. One is getting experience. Experiencing different parts of the world, different points of view and different types of people is essential for broadening your perspective. The other way is to look for disconfirming evidence – this means actively search for it. If something does not go according to plan, find new ways to succeed in your ventures. If someone has an opposing viewpoint to yours, listen to them, and attempt to understand. You might find out something new that you would never have thought of implementing before. Finally, take a look at your business and social circles and find a way to vary them so that you can discover new points of view.

Develop a Mitigation Strategy

Some problems are not as easy to solve as they look to be on the surface. You can find the easy solution and fix it, but in the long run, the real problem will only be solved if you find out the core of the issue and solve it from there. Identifying the core problem involves studying the situation and developing a mitigation strategy.

Broaden Your Set of Experiences

If you ever find yourself stereotyping, or over-genera-lizing based on your own experience, it is because your dataset is too narrow. The best solution to this is to go out of your way to spend time with people who are radically different than you. It might be uncomfortable, or even scary, at first. However, getting a sense of what others think and experience serves as a way for you to gain new experiences that you can use to improve your interactions with others. You should view new experiences as new opportunities. Branch out, listen to alternative viewpoints, and keep a fresh outlook.

Chapter 2.

Intellectual Laziness

Certainly, anyone can learn to think more critically if they put their mind to it and commit to practicing it daily. However, most people do not think critically as much as they think they do. One thing that sabotages critical thinking in anyone is that most people try to avoid thinking.

Put in on a day-to-day basis. There are a few techniques that people employ, so they don't have to think critically as much as they should.

Thinking critically takes a lot of effort, much more effort than most people want to.

Intellectual laziness goes hand-in-hand with passive thinking. It is not thinking critically and not attempting to come to conclusions outside of what you were told. With intellectual laziness, people succumb to the social pressure of what other people around them believe and do not form opinions for themselves.

What often happens is that intellectually lazy people fall into the mindset that someone else cannot disagree with them. However, they are allowed to say whatever they want and offend, insult, and discredit that person for disagreeing with them. Essentially, they have convinced themselves of their own moral and intellectual superiority but are lazy because they refuse to take the time to consider any other point of view.

Chapter 3.

Remember to Start With Reasoning

Sometimes we want to find a solution to make the situation in front of our work. When we do this, we can quickly forget that there are alternatives available to us! Remember to start with reasoning. Don't look at things from your perspective. Consider all avenues of equal importance.

Then, you can form judgments. These judgments should be objective, but they can also be from your perspective. There are a few ways that you can improve your judgment skills. Make sure to recognize the faults of your past to pull valuable information that will keep you from repeating mistakes. You also have to recognize the biases that you experience. These include things such as:

1. Your level of optimism/pessimism.

2. How much you favor a person/place/idea.

3. Your expectancy of an event based on the prob-ability that it has happened in the past.

4. The ability to notice details/larger concepts.

Make an analysis. Were you right / were you wrong? What needs adjusting? Here are your how-to steps of proper analysis:

1. Break it down into pieces to start with one area at a time.

2. Create a goal for what information you'd like to pull.

3. Gather all the important information needed.

4. Make judgments and correct the process to gain desired results.

Finally, you will take away something that you learned from this experience. Even in the most challenging scenarios, there will be something valuable that you can pull.

To increase your ability to do all of these things, you will have to research, practice, research, practice, and repeat over and over again. Practice is something that you have to do on your own, but let's take a look at some other methods of accelerated learning that can help drive your success even further.

Improving Decision-Making and Problem-Solving Skills

The worst thing that tarnishes our ability to make decisions is that we struggle because we are afraid of making the right one. The majority of the stress that we feel comes from being afraid that we might not be making the right one (Chen, Rossignac-Milon, & Higgins, 2018). Decision making isn't an easy process. This is why we often have others decide for us! Think of the last time that you went to the grocery store. Maybe you weren't sure what snack to buy. A display of candy bars or chips that were on sale helped make your decision. Then you got home and plopped in front of the TV, ready to find something good to watch. Rather than scrolling through, you went with the first pick of what was recommended for you. It felt like you made a decision, but most of these choices were made for you throughout the day.

When we struggle to make decisions, we struggle to problem solve as well. If you aren't sure of yourself, don't think critically, and have mental fog, then it will be hard to make a quick decision. Not all problems need instant solutions, but many of us still struggle to come up with the right answer because of all the other thoughts jumbled within our brain. Here, we are going to give you the best decision-making and problem-solving methods so that you can think as fast as possible without letting these processes slow you down.

Making decisions can be hard because there's so much other fluff that can get in the way of clear thinking. Imagine that you are trying to make a cake in your kitchen. If stuff is cooking in the oven, there are dishes in the sink, and another person is trying to make a meal as well, it will be harder to focus on the cake! We have to keep a clear head to make it easier to think quickly. There are a few steps to do this:

1. Prioritize your thoughts.

2. Look at the most basic version of the problem or decision.

3. Analyze to find all possible options.

Let's first take a look at the how-to of prioritizing the most important thoughts.

How to Prioritize Important Thoughts

To work optimally and get the things done that need to be taken care of, you'll want to learn how to prioritize better the things that are most important to you. We often try and do the things that we want to get out of the way at that moment. Maybe you're cleaning your home, and you have to do the dishes, do the laundry, and clean up your room. As you walk throughout the house, however, you see smaller tasks that need to get done, so it's easier to get distracted. What's most important, however, is that we prioritize the things that we initially wanted to get done as they are essential. You didn't think of completing the other tasks until they were right in front of you. So is it all that important to you?

Sometimes everything seems like it is important. Your brain can be very good at convincing you of certain levels of urgency. Anything could be meaningless or dire if you thought about it.

If you have a problem or need to make a decision, there are some prioritization tools that you need. First, write a master list of everything needed to know about this situation. What needs to be done? What are the problems that are going to keep you from completing these tasks?

First, decide the level of importance, how quickly it needs to be done, and the estimated time that it will take to complete. Sometimes you will discover a problem that can be easily taken care of when you can prioritize properly.

You must narrow your options to the very core. You won't be able to make the right decision if you aren't properly prioritizing your thoughts and actions.

Sometimes we struggle to decide because we are scared of what will happen if we don't make the right decision. We don't think about what that worst-case scenario is even going to be! Then, make sure to remind yourself to look at the past and discover that things turned out completely fine. You are OK today, so even when you made the wrong decision, everything ended up working out.

After this, use examples to help you make decisions. If you're stuck, Google your specific question because someone online has likely had the same dilemma. Yahoo Answers, Reddit, and Quora are great user-based tools that many people use to share their struggles online. You can get multiple answers if you ever need more advice than what you are already experiencing.

The best decisions will be made when things are planned out, and you can't do this if you aren't properly planning in the first place! Sometimes we have to make sure that we plan before, rather than waiting until after we face the problem, to make the right decision.

How to Identify the Real Issue

One method for problem-solving is to look at the real issue that needs to be confronted. We often try to find solutions that will help get us out of a situation fast. You might want the quick fix or an easy alternative so that less effort is required. However, if you do try to take shortcuts, it can end up hindering your ability to find a positive solution in the end.

Sometimes, the person making the decision doesn't want to have to admit that they're wrong. Maybe it's a spouse, a boss, or someone else that refuses to accept responsibility for the outcome. What can you do to help get to the root of the issue? How can you find a solution without having to make them feel bad or prove them wrong in the first place?

It is important to train your brain to go directly to the core. Always ask, "Why?" Go through the normal questions of who, what, where, when, and why. Dig deeper and use your critical thinking skills to get you to the real problem that's hidden underneath it all. Think of the last time you had two friends fighting. They might have fought over something small, maybe one was rude to the other, or perhaps there was a little misunderstanding. Between two average individuals, maybe it's not a big deal, but these friends might have blown things out of proportion. Part of this is because there was likely a deeper issue hidden underneath the rest that made everything feel worse than what it was.

To understand how to make the best decisions and come up with the greatest solutions for certain problems, you can use a root-cause analysis. There are a few steps to this process. As an example, we are going to use the idea of someone that struggled to lose weight because the diets they have tried never worked.

First, identify what the issue is at face value. What is the most basic understanding of the problem? In our example, it is that someone struggles to lose weight.

Share this problem with someone else. Discuss it and gain a different perspective. In this example, the person that wants to lose weight might talk to a doctor, nutritionist, or even someone else that shares their struggles.

Look at all the things that could have caused or influenced this issue. This is when thinking becomes deeper. In this example, they struggle because they suffer from anxiety. Their mother was very hard on them about losing weight. They use food as a source of comfort. Exercising is difficult for them.

Come up with a few different solutions. At this point, you can see the many different causes; therefore, you can develop different solutions. In this example, you might talk to a professional about overcoming anxiety, so the emotional eating stops, and they can work through issues with their mother. A better exercise routine can be presented, as well.

Choose the solution that will work best. This would be dependent on the individual, but as you can see, the solutions that we came up with aren't simply "find a new diet plan" because that is not going to solve the root of the problem.

Decide if this was the right thing to do. After this analysis has happened and a solution is chosen, it's time to implement the strategy. The person trying to lose weight can see a therapist and sign up for a yoga class.

Fix and prepare anything else needed for this process. This is when you would reflect and determine if the best course of action had been taken. If weight loss is occurring, then the right solution was found. If no weight loss is happening, it's time to dig deeper or try out a new solution.

Chapter 4.

Improving Your Listening Skills

"Most people do not listen with the intent to understand; they listen with the intent to reply."

– Stephen R. Covey

The Question: "How can I listen in a way that I accurately understand the other person, such that they feel truly heard and understood by me, especially on an emotional topic?"

In every class I've ever taught, and I've taught many and continue to, it's the Listening Skill where the greatest "aha" moments happen for the class participants. Most come to the same realization that I did – that their listening skills have not been very good and can be greatly improved.

As I mentioned earlier, I was trained and certified to teach several communication skills courses. Each course focuses on listening skills in one way or another. It's called by many names – reflective listening, active listening, power listening, etc. In any case, they each highlight the importance of being empathic to the speaker, quieting your mind and putting yourself in their shoes so that you accurately understand them, and they feel understood.

Back From the Brink

I remember one instance at the end of a communication skills class when this young lady, with her husband sitting beside her, stood up and appreciated the course and getting to know everyone and said, "You all didn't know this, but before we came to this class my husband and I decided we had had enough of each other and were going to file for a divorce." This surprised everyone. She continued, "We have three small children, but we felt we just couldn't take it anymore. But after attending this class, and especially learning the listening skills, we both realized we had been poor listeners and misunderstood each other a lot, which just made things worse and worse. We now have a skill that will help us listen better. We have hope now to make a new start together as a couple and family."

This is the power of Empathic Listening – it can help make a healthy relationship even better, and it can help a relationship that's veered off track move back into a positive direction.

Empathic Listening Skill Has 5 Steps

Step 1: Quiet your mind and focus on the other person as they are speaking. Put yourself in their world, look from their point of view.

This means not only being silent and not speaking when the other person is talking but also quieting your mind from distracting thoughts that prevent you from really listening. I've certainly found this to be a challenge myself, and I assume you also have. When the other person is speaking, it's easy to mentally drift away or think, When will they get to the point? Or, I wonder what's for lunch, or glance at the clock on the wall to get the time, etc.

These distractions take us away from being fully present in the here and now and receptive to what the speaker is saying. It takes conscious awareness, self-discipline, and practice to focus correctly and consistently on the other person while they're speaking. We need to remind ourselves throughout the day of its importance and make an effort. As we listen to what the other person is saying, focusing on their underlying feelings about what they're saying, and try to get "locked-in" to their perspective, the peripheral distractions will start to disappear.

Step 2: Without bias, defensiveness, or thinking about what you'll say, listen fully and openly to what they're saying in their words and body language. Listen actively.

Interpersonal communication has been the subject of several research studies over the years. Perhaps not surprisingly, they have concluded that the majority of interpersonal communication is non-verbal, meaning communication is not simply the processing of words. What the research found is that facial expression, body language, tone of voice, posture, eye contact, or lack of it say a lot.

For example, if someone is saying, "You're great," or, "That was a really smart thing to do," but they roll their eyes sarcastically, what are they saying? Something other than what was implied by their words alone. Thus, we might listen more through our eyes than through our ears! All the more reason to listen intently to what the other person is saying and conveying to us. As we do so, we'll more likely to get the full meaning of what they're communicating.

Also, listening without bias or defensiveness or thinking what we'll say comes into play when we may be having a conversation involving high emotions, differences of opinion, or an argument. In those cases, it's easy to slip into preparing our response or rebuttal rather than listening clearly and fully to what the other person is saying.

Here's the Problem

If, for example, you're talking to me about something I disagree with you on, and I'm simply thinking about my response or rebuttal to what you're saying and not fully listening to you, then I might respond to something you didn't say or intend because I wasn't listening!

I've seen this problem with many couples in my classes. Because they didn't listen fully to each other, they often misunderstood what the other was saying and implying, which led to even greater misunderstandings and feelings of hurt, anger, and even resentment – all because they weren't fully listening to each other in the first place.

Often correcting this one thing enabled the couples to communicate much more easily with each other and discuss and work through topics of disagreement much more successfully. Issues that had been hang-ups and huge problems for them were often dealt with and resolved simply by slowing down the process to hear each other fully.

Step 3: Listen "through the words" to the deeper thoughts and feelings that you sense from the speaker.

Keep in mind that emotions are feelings – they are not in word form. When someone wants to express in words what they are feeling (their wants, desires, concerns, etc.), they take those feelings and cycle them through their brain to try to come up with the best words (vocabulary) to explain those feelings coherently. The words they choose and the sentences they say are the best they can come up within the moment. If you listen only to the words, then you might miss a lot of the underlying meaning.

Only a small percentage of an iceberg is above the waterline. Most of it is underneath and unseen. Likewise, if I listen only to the words, you say, and with only my definition of those words, then I might get only a surface understanding of what you're trying to communicate. But if I try to listen through the words to grasp your under-lying meaning and intent of the words, I have a greater chance of getting to and understanding your deeper thoughts and feelings.

For example, if you tell me you just lost your job but that you're confident you'll get another one soon and I only listen to your words, I might conclude that you've only hit a minor bump in the road and you're not too bothered by it. But if I see the worry on your face and hear your wavering tone of voice and listen through the words to the reality that you just lost your primary source of income, that all adds up to me that you're far more concerned about your situation than your surface words of confidence alone would seem to indicate.

Step 4: Don't interrupt them as they are speaking to you or try to finish their sentences. Just listen!

Interrupting other people when they are speaking is a major communication problem. Almost everyone I've known and those I've taught in my classes admit that they sometimes (or often) do this – they think they are show-ing empathy by 'engaging' the speaker by talking while the speaker is talking or they think this will help speed up the conversation.

In one of my women's classes in federal prison, I had the women pair up to have a practice conversation about a person they admire and why. My instruction was that they would choose who would go first, and that person would speak, and their partner would listen intently without interrupting them.

After a few minutes of the first person speaking, I asked the pairs to switch roles so that the speaker became the listener, and the listener became the speaker. After several minutes of doing this, I brought the class back together and asked, "What was that like?" One of the ladies said, "It was so difficult for me not to butt into what she was saying. I'd always thought if we're not both talking at the same time, the other person would think I'm not engaged in the conversation." I asked her partner what it felt like to be listened to without interruption. She smiled and said, "We've been friends for quite a while, and this is the first time I felt she heard everything I wanted to say." They both chuckled, but the message was clear. She finally felt listened to and understood. This was an important lesson for everyone – the power of Empathic Listening.

"Well, let me get there!"

On another occasion, I'll never forget what a pastor's wife said in a small class. I taught a few years ago. It was a class of six pastor couples who had gotten together at a church for communication skills training.

I had just taught them the listening skill when one of the wives turned to her husband (senior pastor of their church) and said, "I'm tired of talking to you!" He looked at her, stunned, and the rest of us were stunned too. He asked, "Why?" and she said, "Every time I try to tell you something, you go and try to finish my sentence!" "Well, I think I know where you're going to go with that," he said, to which she replied, "Well, let me get there!"

Step 5: Say back to them, in your own words, what they said, and their feelings that you sensed from them to make sure you understand them correctly, and they feel understood.

This is a powerful aspect of Empathic Listening. When you say back to the speaker the essence of what you heard them say, this accomplishes two things: 1) it helps confirm that you heard what they said and meant – that you got it correctly and you understand them, and 2) it helps the speaker know what they sounded like, what they communicated. They may think they explained themselves fully, but by your feedback – saying back in your own words what they said – they will know if it was enough or if they need to explain more.

Chapter 5.

By Observing, You Start Changing

Did you know that by simply observing something, you change it? I know that sounds magical, but it's backed up by hard science. In physics, this is called the Heisenberg principle. By simply observing a phenomenon, you change the result.

This also applies to what's going on in your head and your heart. By simply choosing to become aware, you are already starting the process of changing your behavior, the words that come out of your mouth, and, most importantly, your emotional, instinctual responses. The best part of all of this is that you're not trying to reprogram consciously. You're not trying to step in there and move things around. You're not purposefully rearranging your mental furniture. You're not doing any of that. You're just simply allowing yourself to become aware. You're merely choosing to open your eyes to what's going on in your mind, in your heart, and your logical processes. By observing, you start changing.

Observe Without Judging

Try to observe how certain external triggers bring out specific emotional responses in you. Be aware of the connection. Look at what happens outside of you and trace it to your feelings. Keep focusing on this connection. The key here is to observe without judging. You're not saying to yourself, "This is bad. I shouldn't be doing that."

No. You're just looking with curiosity at how certain things bring about particular feelings or specific mental connections. That is the extent of your job at this point. Just observe.

Be Your Mind's Most Avid Student

By simply allowing ourselves to be merely an objective observer, kind of like a foreign exchange student who just got dropped into your mind to pay attention and log what they witness, you will be able to see many things that you're normally blind to. The reason why you're blind to them is not that they don't exist, or that they're hard to see. Instead, you are so focused on judging them that you essentially deal with the stimuli in an unthinking way. You only need to see, for example, certain elements, and you automatically conclude that they mean something. You just take it from there. You run with it.

It's not much different from a hunter going to the forest and seeing a big tail with a bushy end and a lot of hair in the center. The hunter hears a growl. The hunter then puts all these factors together and starts heading the other direction at full speed. Why? The hunter organized all this information and came up with the judgment that there was a lion several yards ahead of them. If that hunter kept going in that direction, the lion might end up enjoying a two-legged lunch item.

We tend to do this and, generally, it works for us. For the most part, we're able to save a lot of valuable mental processing time by just simply looking at a tiny fraction of a larger phenomenon, assuming that it means something, and making decisions. The problem is if you want to overcome your negative narratives, you have to connect the dots directly. You have to override your habit of jumping to conclusions.

Connecting the Dots?

Let's just get one thing out of the way. You're already connecting the dots. By and large, this is the reason why you're having a tough time. This mental activity is the reason why you're having issues with depression, anxiety, worry, and limiting beliefs that undermine self-esteem and self-confidence. You are doing too much dot-connecting.

Now, I'm going to ask you to be aware of how you normally connect the dots and see the gaps there. The reason why you feel that there are certain negative areas in your life is that at some level or other, you're connecting the dots in one specific way. Maybe it's time to reconnect the dots, coming up with new connections and fresh patterns.

Unfortunately, there is no one-size-fits-all formula for this. You have to do it yourself based on your particular set of data. Everybody's triggers are different. Everybody's objective pieces of information are distinct. Still, we all do this. This is one of the few things we all have in common. The difference, however, is the fact that some connections are more productive than others.

You need to look at how you're constantly concluding these stimuli based on your narratives. Pay attention to how this choice leads you to act a certain way. After

31

becoming aware that this is going on, start reconnecting the dots. Do you think that you could have a better result if you connected your past experiences and personal narratives with triggers a different way?

See the Overall Pattern of Your Life

The reason why automatic behaviors and seemingly self-regulating emotional states seem almost irresistible is that they are set patterns. We feel we can't escape them. However, keep in mind that you are living in a personal prison of which you are the warden. You're the gate-keeper. You have the keys in your hand. The reason why you're staying in that fixed range of options is that you choose to.

Remember, you chose all these narratives at some level or other. It's like living in prison, and you have the keys in your hand. You see the keys every single day. You see them so often that they seem like they're not there. But they're still there in your hand. You could always choose to go about doing things differently.

Your narratives, when woven together, form your lifestyle. We all have a distinct lifestyle-a distinct way of living. Our narratives power it.

Is the pattern clear yet? Your normal tendency to connect certain dots and leave particular dots unconnected will produce your lifestyle. Your lifestyle then produces your life. Understand how your narratives work through this process. Get familiar with how they flow into each other. Finally, understand how they define you.

The More Aware You Are, the More You Can Change Yourself

As I said, the great news is that by simply being aware, you start changing things in your life. The longer you observe how you behave and how you interpret certain segments of reality to mean specific things, the more power you will have over your 'automatic' thoughts and actions. The more you understand which triggers unleash certain emotional states and how these lead to certain actions, the more you can change yourself.

Be aware that this is happening. Become aware that you're connecting certain dots. Be aware that you believe specific patterns are true, and this defines your identity.

Don't Take Things for Granted

Now, just as you can be looking at a particular phenomenon out in the natural world, it's easy to take certain things for granted. It's so comfortable to think that once you see exact things, then it's easy to conclude specific truths.

On the flip side, if you feel that you don't see certain things, then it is okay not to conclude a certain truth. You should stop thinking in terms of shorthand, and instead choose to look at all the things that are playing out in these patterns with a fresh set of eyes. Allow yourself to question everything. Don't just go by assumption.

Don't take things for granted. Don't be fatalistic and assume that there's not much you can do about the things going on in your life. Don't be dismissive, either. Don't think that just because certain things are there or they're not there, then they don't mean that much. Instead, look at everything that is happening and see its value. Try to uncouple each element in your assumptions or disconnect it from whatever it is normally attached to and try to come up with new connections.

For example, if memories of your father constantly trigger you because you did not have a good relationship with him, don't automatically recoil at the memory of certain words or phrases from your father.

For instance, my friend Adam was always told by his dad that he was an idiot. Adam rebelled against his father by smoking a lot of weed when he was a teenager. In college, he ended up doing a lot of drugs. After graduating, he simply chose to coast through life. He didn't have much drive. He didn't apply himself.

I lost touch with Adam for several decades. Intrigued by CBT, he let me walk him through key memories and coping mechanisms he had. I was able to work with Adam to the point where he was able to take the emotional sting out of the memories he had about his father. When he remembers his father calling him an 'idiot' or saying he's 'good for nothing, he now has a different interpretation.

I worked with Adam to re-interpret that memory as his father challenging him to be better than what he was settling for. Because Adam was one of those "super genius" kids in junior high, he was always easily bored. When a teacher introduced a new concept, Adam figured it out backward and forwards before the teacher could even fully explain it. That's how quick Adam's mind was. And accordingly, he got bored easily. And he would always take the easy way out and do as little as possible to challenge himself.

Perhaps his father, when he told Adam, "You're an idiot," was saying that out of love, or out of frustration over the fact that this young person was capable of so much more but constantly contented himself with doing the very least. When we looked at that alternative meaning and we 're-connected' many of his other memories to his narratives, Adam's demeanor changed. All that anger and that free-floating frustration that he had with his father started to melt away.

After six months, I met up with Adam again, and he had launched a start-up Internet company that had just been founded a few million dollars. He said to me that our talks about his father had shown him that he could expect greater things from himself. Our conversations changed him, as well as his whole relationship with the concept of ambition and how he defined personal ambition.

It truly blew my mind that Adam had come up with this amazing idea for a mobile app that is extremely exciting as far as personal productivity and commercial applications go. He had success in him all this time. Still, for the longest time, he chose to interpret his father's statements about him in such a way that it dragged him down, instead of pushing him upward and forward to his fullest potential.

This is what happens when we allow ourselves to avoid being fatalistic and dismissive when we're looking at the dots in our narratives. They may seem like they've been there for a long time. They may seem all too 'natural.' They may even seem logical. Regardless, there are always other interpretations. Never lose sight of these. Don't be dismissive. Don't think that just because your emotional roller coaster operates one way for so long, you're stuck with it.

Chapter 6.

Managing Your Feelings

Managing feelings is strongly a matter of choice. Want to, or don't you? So much has been published regarding feelings and how to cope successfully with them, and a lot of people cannot regulate this aspect of life. Why? For what? Effectively controlling feelings is like cultivating an ability or a pattern. It's a chance to do something different, and we as people struggle the most with the transition.

It is not easy to change the way you normally do something, and it is much tougher when it comes to feelings. If we feel' emotional,' the last thing we want to do is cool down and try and pro-actively deal with the situation; most of the time, we want to freak out about what upsets us.

When we learn a little more about how our feelings function, then we are in a lot better position to make use of this knowledge. Understanding how to control your emotions can be one of the best skills in your life that you will ever create. Your feelings contribute to the acts you are doing and thereby build the life you are now experiencing, every aspect of it.

Our cognitive part of the brain, the limbic region, is one of the oldest components of contrast, for instance, with our prefrontal cortex, which is our area of thought. Since our emotional part is so ancient, and hence an extremely strong part of the brain, it is normal that it seems like our feelings often rule us and hijack our minds. The emotional part of the normal person's brain is more than six billion times more powerful than the prefrontal cortex. The argument is your feelings can hijack your thinking – this is a given – but there are still ways to deal with that.

Let's look at what you can do to turn the scenario around to keep things simple. Ignoring or not coping with thoughts will come back to bite you! Stress and fear stem from feelings that have been suppressed, and if you believe it is going to help to cope with the emotions by suppressing them, you are sadly wrong.

Four Simple Steps to Control Your Emotions

1. The First Step Is Awareness

If you don't recognize the moments when you're overly emotional or over-reacting, how can you handle it? It couldn't be. Start tracking the thoughts and give them names. Even we find it hard to define what we mean. Giving it a name allows us to gain insight, which is key to development.

2. Discover the 'Why' of Your Emotions

Once you've figured out how you feel, you want to find out why you feel it. Friend, "What is wrong? What is it that makes me feel this way?"Your mind will always look for an answer.

Most of the time, simply the way you are thinking about the situation is causing you to feel the way you do

3. Then Ask Yourself, "What Is the Solution?"

Upon figuring out why, what can you do to take back control? You may need to change the way you think about the case often. Your emotions lead directly to your feelings, you see, so if you feel bad, you will most definitely have a negative thought that makes you feel that way. When you start talking of some different forms of looking at the situation, you'll instantly start feeling better. What you're focused on grows! Often your feelings can continue to decrease simply from knowing that you feel a certain way at a certain moment and understanding often contributes to relaxing.

4. Choose How You Want to React

This is the most difficult part. One pattern is how we respond and control our emotions. Have you not seen those people who are stressing out, practically flipping out over nothing? You feel almost sorry for them. We have developed a culture of associating with' freaking out' a circumstance we do not like. Their feelings have invaded them.

It's not something you plan to do twice a week at lunchtime and learn to listen to your thoughts, to recognize, appreciate, and then choose them. No, you can start building the essential skill with continuous effort and discipline.

Five Proven Habits to Help Manage Your Emotions

Emotions often become the most traumatic force of our existence. The feelings guide us in our everyday lives. Our feelings control our emotions. But mostly we operate on our emotions very easily and often make decisions that we regret in our life by operating on the wrong kind of emotions. But some individuals do exceptionally well in controlling their feelings. We simply stop working on the incorrect kinds of thoughts, and in the most complicated situations, control their emotions. Then are the few measures to better regulate impulses and restore composure in stressful situations.

1. Set Healthy Boundaries

The best way to keep the emotions under control is to establish healthy boundaries for people and ideas that exceed our physical and emotional limitations. Only resolve not to allow a person or negative emotion to manipulate our weaker selves and reject our principles.

2. Get to the Root Cause

Anger or sorrow lies deeper than we see on the surface. Those who control their feelings quickly get to the root cause of what disturbs them, according to experts. They are being truthful with themselves and knowing what can trouble them. They effectively repair their issues after some processing.

3. Think Over a Situation

Those with well-controlled feelings don't respond to things but worry about them instead. We have their perspective, listen without judgment, and stop the immediate reaction. We can do the same by distancing ourselves from the circumstance that can cause our emotions. We must be self-conscious about the potential consequences of losing the influence of our feelings.

4. Take Time to Pause

Emotions are required to soar during a dispute. When we stop for a while, the influx of chemicals being generated slows down and lets us easily determine the action's costs and benefits.

5. Reach Out First After an Argument

People reach out to be the first one to make amends and save their relationships. That is what we should also do in our lives. When we reach out to those we have had a harsh conversation with, it will do wonders for our relationship.

Empathy

Empathy is the capability of comprehending other individual's feelings. It is also vital to emotional intelligence but provides more insight to an individual rather than recognizing the emotions of others. Empathy involves realizing emotions as well as reactions to these emotions, which primarily encompasses the help needed. For example, if someone is hopeless, sad, or emotionally dependent, you are likely to sense these emotions and respond accordingly as if they are yours. You tend to provide extra care and concern, allowing other people to recognize power dynamics that influence relationships. Therefore, emotional intelligence enables you to become empathetic to others and give the needed support.

Intrinsic Motivation

Unlike others, people with emotional intelligence abilities are rarely motivated by external rewards, for example, richness, fame, or acclaim. These people usually work to meet their personal needs and objectives. They seek to ensure their internal satisfaction which, in turn, leads to rewarding their inner needs. Such individuals remain action-oriented by creating goals that are of higher standards and work to achieve. Also, they remain committed to performing their duties entirely when needed without failure. As such, the motivation allows for the achievement of essential goals in nearly everything they engage in, no matter the complexity of the situation.

More Emotional People

More emotional people tend to have low emotional intelligence and therefore, become very reactive, especially on negative emotions. In this case, these people usually lack self-awareness, self-regulation, and other components of emotional intelligence. When someone is regarded as a more sensitive person, the chances are that they may become very reactive on occasions such as anger and become violent. When sad, they may end up becoming stressed, lonely, and eventually, being depressed. This group of people may, however, have some ability to control some of their emotions but limited knowledge about how they react to a given situation.

More emotional people may, at times, face difficulties on how they interact publicly, henceforth, cannot sustain relationships. Some of the characteristic features of more emotional people include the inability to understand other people's emotions, getting into arguments quickly, blaming others for their mistakes, and lack of empathy. Other features include difficulty sustaining friends, sudden outbursts of emotions, refusal to listen to other's views, and thinking people are usually oversensitive. More emotional people typically have no control over how they express their feelings or emotions. Therefore, they become too dependent on themselves without minding others.

Less Emotional People

Less emotional people are those individuals with the ability to control their emotions or feelings even when they are profound or negative. These individuals usually have a much higher emotional intelligence when compared to more emotional people. As highlighted above, less emotional people can suppress their emotions even in the states where these emotions seem unbearable. They may look calm and in peace even after a hurtful event. More so, they are relaxed and understanding and interact well with the general public, mainly with friends, family, and those close to them, such as coworkers.

When in an emotional state, for instance, these individuals typically respond to issues rather than react and understand the matter at hand. They are equipped with the components of emotional intelligence as well as self-control and handle situations with their related selves. When faced with a more challenging situation, less emotional people rarely complain but work to find ways of solving the problem, which, in most cases, succeed with limited failure possibilities. As typical human beings, however, less emotional people also undergo similar impacts of negative emotions. Still, due to their emotional intelligence abilities, they readily get in control of their feelings and find ways to handle these situations without causing scenes.

Chapter 7.

Self-Awareness

Emotional self-consciousness is an ongoing focus on one's internal states, including emotions. It's a neutral state that, even though intense emotions, continues self-examination.

Self-awareness is the same for practical purposes, and the ability to change our moods. Emotions can be unconscious and often are. They start before a person becomes consciously aware of that feeling. There are thus two levels of sentiment, conscious and unconscious. Unconscious emotions can have a powerful impact on thoughts and reactions, even if we don't know them. When we become aware of them, we can evaluate them. Self-awareness is thus the basis on which to manage emotions and be able to shake off a bad mood.

Know Yourself

You have to know what to work with before you can make changes within yourself. Becoming self-aware is about getting yourself understood.

Emotional awareness means being able to recognize the emotions you are experiencing, understand the emotion-related feelings, and understand what you think and do as a result.

Professional athletes get intensive training to help them recognize and overcome their emotions.

They mustn't allow frustration or anger to affect their performance.

You'll be more positive about what you can and cannot do when you're aware of your strengths and limitations. Self-confident people are more assertive about what they think is right.

Being assertive does not mean that you are always getting your way, but rather that you are firmly conveying your thoughts and ideas and defending why you think that a particular decision or suggestion is the right one.

The competencies associated with self-consciousness are:

- Emotional self-consciousness: recognizing your emotions and their impact on your life.

- Precise self-assessment: identify strengths and limitations.

- Trust in oneself: knowing one's self-worth and abilities.

Values, Beliefs, and Assumptions

Values are the principles that guide our lives, standards, morals, ethics, and ideals. Knowing your values is an important part of building self-awareness.

Assumptions

One important aspect of emotional intelligence is developing an awareness of the assumptions we hold about others. Self-awareness also means we're not supposed to ignore the assumptions we hold about ourselves.

We can have positive or negative beliefs about ourselves. Negative assumptions involve thoughts like' I still happen bad things to me' or' I don't know enough to start my own business.' Positive assumptions could include thoughts like' If I keep trying, I'll be successful' or' Inherently good people.

Spend some time concentrating on a challenging task you recently accomplished. Do you think of a single one? It may be related to work or something that you did at home.

What were your first thoughts regarding your ability to complete the task?

If your initial thoughts were negative about yourself, that's fine! But spend some time thinking about how those thoughts made you feel about the task being completed. How could you turn that thought around? Take a moment to write down a more favorite positive thought that you may try at another time.

The beliefs we hold about ourselves are important as they decide our actions.

"Having more self-awareness or understanding means getting a better grasp of reality."

– Dalai Lama

Self-consciousness is the basic building block for emotional intelligence. It's a journey to become self-aware, and we'll probably spend a lifetime learning about ourselves. But as we improve self-awareness, we are also enhancing our life experience, creating opportunities for a better work-life balance, becoming aware of our emotions, and improving our ability to respond to change.

Show or Feel What You Are Feeling

Being familiar with emotion is not the same as having it expressed. We can make a sensible choice about how to respond or whether to respond at all, but only if we are aware of the emotions we are experiencing can we make those choices. The knowledge opens up new behavioral possibilities.

Not being aware of our "self," when someone "pushes our buttons" can also cause us trouble. We blow up out of percentage to the position because a limbic memory has been triggered. Perhaps we revert to responses experienced in childhood – shrinking when a boss yells at us, maybe because of an old memory of verbal abuse. Being self-conscious is the key to self-control and freedom of action; empathy and true human connection can come out of it.

Sometimes, we don't know what we feel until the feelings become quite intense. However, the truth is that we always feel something as we always think something. If we want to advance in intelligence, we need to pay more attention to the process of cognition. If we want to become more emotionally intelligent, we need to be careful and let ourselves feel real. Tuning toward our physical self is where self-awareness has to start.

Serious physical or emotional trauma can cause an individual to "turn off" their awareness of what is happening to them — a way of coping with it that can become an emotional "handicap" carried into adulthood that stifles ability and potential leadership. The damage can be fixed through positive adult relationships, a desire to change, and therapy. Adult brains with persistence and patience can relearn emotional patterns.

The Language of Feelings

Which words do you use to describe your feelings? Many people cannot give their feelings labels outside a few straightforward ones, such as anger, worry, sadness, or happiness. (The' negative' emotions are those we seem to remember, no matter what!) Since self-awareness is an essential part of Emotional Intelligence and being in touch with what we feel is critical to self-awareness, we need a language or framework to describe our emotions comfortably.

Emotional energy can grow, give us a push, or contract, pulling us back. Because there are many billions of neural pathways, there are many possible combinations, subtleties, and synonyms of the basic emotions.

How Emotions Manifest Themselves?

When, without better communication, we do not pay attention to emotions and know how to mark and cope with them, they manifest themselves in the body: exhaustion, lack of concentration, discomfort, and poor health. When we concentrate on emotions and slowly encourage ourselves to experience them, they will increase in strength and help us to learn and communicate with other people.

Recommendations for Increasing Self-Awareness

Look inward. We are assaulted with messages about the outside world, and within ourselves, we still struggle to connect with the universe. Here are some ways of understanding who we are:

1. Hold a journal; Try to write on a specific question too: "What's important to me? "After writing on this topic for several days, start asking yourself:" Is it how I spend my time reflecting on what is important to me?

2. As a clue to your passions, get in touch with your work preferences. Work to become part of those activities that you love, instead of just taking on any project. If you've lost touch to the extent that you no longer remember what you love, write about what you've loved in the past.

3. Be conscious of where you feel an emotion in your body: your shoulders, neck, throat, jaw, abdomen, and chest. If you adjust to your physical replies, you can guide the energy and respond flexibly, instead of being in the emotional grip. We want its intensity to get the most out of our energy, but we shouldn't let it control us.

4. Develop a habit of self-observation and self-curiosity: Visualize yourself as if you were looking at a third person. Think about thinking your way. Instead of

allowing yourself to operate on autopilot, tune in with yourself and your emotional stream of consciousness and thus identify your subtle mood.

5. Make yourself spend about self-reflection and awareness-building 15 to 20 minutes a day. Record this in your planner, and don't let it interfere with other things. Do something peaceful, pleasant, and calming, like a quiet stroll, and let your mind wander at will.

6. Think ahead about two situations you will encounter during the day during your commute to work: one that will not produce strong emotions, and another that will result in some emotion.

Pay attention to yourself as you live the experience of every situation: How do you react? What happens in the body and the head? Keep a small log at your writing desk for at least two weeks, and write down information about each of these areas as they relate to a particular situation:

- Heart rate
- Breathing
- Perspiration
- Muscle tightness
- Feelings

7. When you feel tension or low energy, fix it straight away. Take some bites of a healthy snack (junk food doesn't count!), get some fresh air, take a little walk for a change of scenery, stand up and shrug your shoulders and stretch a couple of times, or do some twisting. We need a two to three-minute creative pause every 20 to 30 minutes to keep the energy high.

8. Increasing self-awareness means you'll also become more aware of the "bad stuff," things you don't like about yourself in particular. Challenges and issues are normal, so accept the fact that you will never be sufficiently wise and powerful enough to eliminate flaws.

Being self-conscious means you can turn it into a challenge when you have a problem—and an opportunity to grow. Here are some ideas:

- Defining your problem with great care. Ask yourself, what exactly is happening here?

- Brainstorm new solutions (often with useful elements), including stupid ones.

- Weigh up the pros and cons of your thoughts. Consider equilibrating the brain and heart. What does your spirit, or "healthy" say to you? Is your alternative something you can commit your entire being to? Facts and figures are not the only material things.

- Live for a while with your preferred solution, instead of jumping into immediate action. Let your intuition take over, and have your plan incubated for a few days. If you're still committed with your heart and head, then take action. Evaluate how this will work as you implement your plan, and only modify it as needed.

Chapter 8.

Communication in the Workplace

Communication in the workplace means that you are communicating with people whom you have professional relationships with. A professional relationship is very much different than close relationships like friendships and familial relationships. A professional relationship is an ongoing interaction between two individuals that follows a set of established boundaries that are deemed appropriate under their governing standards. The ability to establish professional relationships is the backbone of a person's career development.

Professional relationships consist of many different types. The most common one that people may think of is the relationship that they have with their manager or boss. Or if you are that manager or boss, then professional relationships are the ones you have with your employees. However, professional relationships have many more types than that. Think doctor to patient relationships, lawyer to client, teacher to student, service provider to the customer, and so on. Professional relationships function in a manner that is very different from friendships and family relationships. Although most professional relationships still have a strong element of friendliness, not many people would consider their doctor their 'friend.'

Professional relationships are one of the most common types of relationships that people struggle with. This is because of how unique it is to the other different types of relationships. If we think about friendships, familial relationships, and romantic relationships, the common element between these three is a level of closeness. When it comes to professional relationships, it is almost forbidden to nurture that sense of closeness. When two people in a professional relationship grow close, it may evolve into a friendship which overpowers the professional relationship.

Many people have to re-learn their communication skills and techniques solely for professional relationships. Although there isn't a universal mandate for how people should communicate in professional environments, there is a loose structure of how people should act. So why do people give professional relationships so much importance? Why do people take courses or read about how to build better professional relationships?

Rather than spending time and energy dealing with problems caused by negative relationships, we can simply just focus on our work and opportunities. Good professional relationships are also extremely necessary if you are hoping to develop your career. If your boss or manager doesn't trust you or even like you, then it is highly unlikely that he/she will consider you for a promotion. Overall, people simply want to work with people that they are on good terms with.

Communication With Romantic Partners/Interests

Communication skills literally can make or break your romantic relationships. Let's take a look at how having a good (or bad) communication skills can impact your relationships.

If you are a good communicator, this means you can:

1. Listen effectively and actively.

2. Observe your thoughts and feelings.

3. Know when a response is not needed.

4. Observe other people and practice empathy.

5. Form thoughtful and appropriate responses according to your observations of yourself and others, through empathy.

By being able to do all of these things, you can connect with people on a deeper level through understanding. You can share information with people effectively and receive information as well. These five points are beneficial in all types of relationships. Relationships are all about connection, and the connection is difficult without the ability to be a good communicator.

If you are a person who struggles with good communication, you may find it difficult to interact with people in professional and personal settings. If you are not able to listen to the people around you and are unable to express yourself through verbal communication, then reaching mutual understanding in your relationships will prove quite difficult. Being able to observe your thoughts and feelings and explain these to other people through writing or speaking, for example, is very important, and being unable to or ineffective at this can lead to miscommunications or misunderstandings in your relationships.

Bad communication is not always in the form of mean words being exchanged or voices being raised. In most cases, bad communication is a lack of communication. When certain things are not acknowledged or said, both people begin to assume things about one another, and conclusions will be drawn. To avoid having bad communication in relationships, over-communication should be used instead. By over-communicating your intentions and your thoughts, the receiving person begins to get an understanding of your style of communication and thought processes. The more they learn about what goes on in your head, the less they will misinterpret you.

This is especially important at the beginning of relationships, as that's where the biggest learning curve is. This holds not only for romantic relationships, but for professional, personal, and familial relationships as well. Just like how you probably have a strong understanding of the way your best friend thinks and communicates, you should know that you have a weak understanding of the way your new coworker thinks and feels and vice versa. To avoid any misunderstandings and arguments, be sure to over-communicate to leave no room for misinterpretations. Once you and the other person have developed an understanding, the two of you can form your style of communication that works for both parties.

Public Speaking

Public speaking is often done by people who want to influence and persuade. They are likely natural leaders who have mastered the art of communication. This does not mean they don't feel anxious or nervous before a public speech. It just means that they feel are confident in their skills to pull it off. To help you with public speaking, we will have to increase your confidence around it. Let's take a look at how learning to persuade and influence people can help you improve our confidence around public speaking.

Being a good public speaker involves some degree of influence and persuasion. When it comes to the type of leadership where there is a vote that decides who the leader will be, persuasion and influence become very important as you will need to get as many people as you can to put their trust in you and select you and what you represent or stand for. Persuasion does not have to include being untruthful, as there are many ways to identify if someone is untruthful.

There are other situations where we may want to be influential that does not involve a vote or that are not political. You may be a parent who needs to influence their child to choose something, or you may want to persuade your friend to make a certain choice. These techniques are still relevant to these types of situations as well.

Appearing confident in your position is crucial when it comes to being persuasive. Just as mentioned, appearing confident in large part depends on your nonverbal communication. If you think and act like a leader in any situation, you will be more convincing and believable to people regardless of if they know you personally or not.

Chapter 9.
Conflict Resolution

When you put more than one person into a room, there can be conflict. Expect it and be ready for it. If you find that two or more members of your team disagree on something, you need to resolve it because this will hold up results and cause a lack of motivation. No one likes going into work knowing that there's a personality clash waiting for them, so you need to decide on how to deal with the situation. Here are some alternatives:

- An open meeting with the whole team.

- A meeting with the members of the team who disagree.

- Changing roles of members, so that clashing members do not work together.

The last option really should be the last thing that you consider. If you do not want to involve others in the problems that are ensuing between two or more members of the team, then the best bet is to call the problematic members to a team meeting that excludes others who are not yet demotivated.

There are some points that you need to remember when it comes to solving conflicts in the workplace. By following these six points, you are setting you and your team up for successful and effective conflict resolution.

1. Make Sure That Good Relationships Are a Priority

Ensure that everyone is being treated with respect. Do what you can to be courteous and to discuss matters constructively. As a leader, it is your responsibility to take and maintain control of the situation and ensure everyone walks away with a positive attitude toward one another.

2. Set People Apart From Problems.

Recognize that, in most cases, the other person is not being difficult. There are real and valid differences lying between the different positions. Separating people from the problems helps you to discuss issues without damaging relationships. Addressing the problem at hand, rather than the personalities of the people involved, ensures that each party will walk away with their self-esteem intact.

3. Pay Attention to a Difference in Interests

By trying to understand the point of view of each person in conflict, you will get a better grasp of why someone has adopted the view that he or she has. Ask for everyone's view on the situation and reiterate that you need everyone's cooperation to resolve the issue. Request that everyone approach the situation with an open mind to learn to understand where others are coming from, whether they agree or not. Once everyone knows their opinion matters as much as the person beside you, they are more likely to be receptive to solving the problem as a group.

4. Listen First, Talk Second

As a manager, set the example by listening to everyone's perspective, and encourage everyone else to do the same without interrupting to defend themselves. By allowing each person to voice their ideas, you are opening yourself and others to possibilities that may have been overlooked in the process of feeling like someone's opinion is greater than another.

5. Set Out the "Facts"

Decide on what facts might impact your decision. This is something that you should be doing together as a team. Sometimes, people are going to see different, although interlocking problems. If you aren't able to reach an agreement on what the problem is, aim to understand the other person's perception of the problem.

6. Explore Options Together

Be open to the idea that a third position may exist and that you might reach it jointly. Ask each team member to help generate solutions, as doing this is going to ensure that everyone feels included. Therefore, they are more likely to be satisfied with the solution.

We are going to cover each of these ideas a little more in-depth eventually.

You do need to talk about the problems and let each member who argues speak in turn to tell you what the problem is from his or her point of view. Do not allow interruption and tell each member of the team that is present at the meeting that each of you must get the problem off your chest so that you are in a position to do something to help the situation. Explain that personality problems or conflict problems do need to be brought to a head because it is affecting the team as a whole and is making everyone unhappy and less productive.

Listen to what your team members say. Perhaps they have a great idea and feel that they are being held back because of what other members of the team have been asked to do. Perhaps jobs overlap, and it hasn't been made clear who should do which part of the job. Remember to point out to the team that you need honest answers as to what's going wrong so that you can appraise the situation and do something about it, and never be afraid to take a little of the blame yourself.

"Perhaps some of this is my fault for having jobs that overlap, and we need to look at that."

"Perhaps we need to talk about changes that will help you all to be the most productive."

Remember that people who have conflict will not be very happy. You need to see what's wrong from every perspective. Although some team leaders do see everyone separately to assess conflicts, I always think that the most adult way to deal with these is to have everyone in the same room and be ready to address the problems that they have. In one team that I led, it seemed that two people needed access to one terminal. Because of the concentrated nature of the task, the terminal was never free for employee B, given that employee A had too much to do and needed to be on that terminal. That was my fault. I should have gauged the situation better, and simply providing employee B with an alternative terminal helped the situation and mended the relationship between both team members. I explained how intense the research that employee A was doing was so that employee B didn't carry on thinking that employee A was just being pedantic and difficult. They still work together today and occasionally have disputes, but nothing that impedes the flow of a job because they are more professional and know how to get around problems of that nature.

One of your jobs as a team leader is to lead, and that means being able to step in and tell people when they are out of line. Be very sure of your footing when you do this, as there may be reasons. It is better to hear their side of the story before leaping in and making mistakes. One employee looked like he did very little for a project, but the fact was that others just made more noise about what they did. This member who didn't move from his desk throughout the project was doing very important work behind the scenes but not making a great deal of fuss about it like the others. When I added up productive hours lost on the job, it wasn't the quiet guy who was responsible. It was those who made the most noise about the work they were doing but who were producing less work than him.

Personalities are difficult to deal with sometimes, but in one project that I ran, emotions were running far too high, and team members were starting to get personal with each other. I closed the office door, called everyone to the center of the room, and told the team that we were not leaving the room until tempers had been cleared up and the frustrations of members had been voiced out. They did a very good job of demonstrating to each other how futile the whole dispute was and came away from the meeting feeling like they had been heard. That's important, but it is also important to remember that the project is everything and that each of your team members needs to be giving it everything he or she has rather than wasting time on personal squabbles. In this case, there was a lot of shouting done by certain members of the team, but bringing it to a head was probably the best move under the circumstances because it managed to get them all to see the futility of all of their arguments when compared with the importance of the job. Conflict resolution is something that can show your skills as a leader. Never lose your temper. Never take sides. Always see the bigger picture, and help your team see it, too. Once you side with a particular member of staff, you may lose the respect of others. Thus, stay professional and neutral to work out the problems and find solutions.

Conflict resolution can also come with benefits. When you solve conflicts effectively, you will proactively and perhaps unknowingly address any other issues that may have resulted from a single conflict. Below are other positive outcomes of conflict resolution:

Increased understanding: conflict resolution will allow awareness and understanding to shine through while making others realize that they do not need to undermine someone else to achieve their own goals.

Improved group cohesion: knowing that there is an effective way to work through disagreements allows team members to feel as though they can be open with one another, garnering mutual respect among team members. This reinforces the idea that a diverse group can effectively work together, even in the face of adversity.

Expanded self-knowledge: when faced with a challenge, people are forced to examine their thoughts, goals, and processes. This helps them realign their priorities and set their focus back to the task at hand.

Though there are benefits to conflict, the very nature of conflict implies there may be damaging outcomes. Knowing how to handle these disagreements effectively will keep people engaged in their work, self-assured, and confident in their group.

When You Can't Solve a Conflict

You might find that in some instances, the disagreement between two people cannot be solved by using any of the methods we have already looked at. In these cases, it might be necessary to separate the parties who are involved in the conflict, so they are working on different teams or different projects. Sometimes, just some time away from one another is enough for your team members to see that they were difficult and unwilling to see the other person's side of things. These team members are often able to move forward and work together in the future.

In some extreme cases, you might find that one of the people in the conflict is trying to work it out, but the other person is, indeed, just being difficult. Sometimes, this is something personal between the two team members, and other times, it could be that the person being difficult has a negative personality. In these cases, it might be necessary to move the difficult team member to a different department to eliminate contact or even let this person go from the company completely. While this is a hard decision to make, you sometimes need to just do the right thing for your team and the organization.

Chapter 10.
Emotionally Intelligent Leaders

Emotional intelligence requires a range of abilities that help us interpret, understand, and affect our emotions and others. Workplaces that either do not have or do not allow workers to apply these skills are not fun workplaces. They are doubtful to be as successful or profitable in the long run because the individuals in the company never really interconnect and operate together. For long-term sustainability, businesses need leaders that empower people, bind with employees 'hearts and minds. Such companies need emotionally wise leaders.

Emotionally intelligent leaders are associated with the people around them. We view them as genuine and empathetic, able to exercise expansionary thinking, always trying to incorporate and appreciate instead of rejecting and dismissing them. It requires a strong and supportive leadership who does not hate other viewpoints and does not have the need to make the definitive decision or to show it is right.

The problem is – who do we know as we talk about our own socially aware leadership experiences? The unfortunate fact is that there's a relative shortage of these people, at least for most of us in the areas where we work. Many organizations also think of thoughts and feelings as valuable and praise people not for WHY but for WHAT outcomes they produce.

The positive thing is that emotionally wise executives are "out there," and several organizations are now involved in helping and promoting these individuals. Such businesses are not a trail of creativity and cutting-edge research. You also agree that there is a more natural way to do it. We recognize that designing a successful workforce is possible and that the assessment and development of the skills needed are far from rocket science, a process that has been tried and tested for years.

Many organizations aim to define and improve the five behaviors common to all emotionally informed leaders. We are:

- Perceive their thoughts and understand them.

- Show easily how they behave.

- 'Tune in' to others thoughts and impulses.

- Send truth and emotions fantastic performance.

- Our own and other emotions are strongly affected.

Intelligent leaders understand and comprehend their feelings: Wise leaders of the emotions understand how incidents and causes contribute to emotional reactions in the workplace. Such emotional responses are founded on biases developed by a mixture of their perceptions, convictions, and values. You learn how this mixture of beliefs and loose array of information influences you, your behavior, whether this impact stays unregulated, and what such conducts and feelings will do for the individuals you deal with.

The consequence of this experience is that they are mindful of the influence their thoughts and desires have on their thought processes, which helps them to reduce the periods that they work successfully. This unfailingly strengthens their decision-making. You have become more associated with their workers by knowing their own feelings and how you express themselves.

For example, take the encounter we have all had with the boss who is inflamed because the problem is not answered. For one time or another, we needed to share negative news-so it doesn't help if we know that the receiver will either turn red or leap to conclusions. Emotionally informed leaders understand what things cause intense feelings and realize when. This helps them to convey their emotions appropriately, approach the situation more constructively and, above all, avoid making a negative effect on the workers that first of all, gave them the issue.

Emotionally intelligent leaders accurately communicate how they feel: emotionally smart leaders are best prepared to talk from the awareness of their own emotions. This skill helps them to help us understand and make choices while still being more honest about the people with whom they interact.

This strengthened emotional communication enhances trust and shared empathy with its peers, which contributes to expanded collaboration. Rather than being viewed as "vulnerable," these leaders capture hearts and minds with sufficient integrity. The objective here is that they learn to speak correctly, to the right degree, at the right time and with the right people.

The benefits of a person who can articulate himself correctly are equal. Second, there are no surprises, and people know where they are with these men. This decreases 'avoiding' habits significantly and promotes open dialogue. Secondly, their integrity helps everyone in the organization to appreciate and view their choices more effectively. This will include staff involved in these actions and raise the likelihood that they will be implemented completely and correctly.

Emotionally wise executives 'tune' to other people's thoughts and emotions: the market is about men-and he couldn't have been perfect. Emotionally aware leaders know that this is completely real and, therefore, 'tune' to their people's thoughts and desires, empathize with them, and try to learn what inspires and energizes them. Such members spend time learning how their constituents think and feel, and above all, spend time explaining and constructively using this understanding.

Such activities build positive working interactions between workers and corporate leaders. These are the ties that form the foundation of a highly motivated and dedicated workforce. The deep interpersonal bond between an individual and a leader is also beyond their commitment to the entire company-even as their inspiration by a caring, and the motivating leader often goes far beyond the encouragement offered by any amount of incentive or threat of discipline.

Emotionally informed leaders balance information and emotions to achieve successful results: psychologically wise leaders will make better decisions by incorporating what they know with how they and others are thinking by being more open and welcoming. It helps us to create more successful partnerships, play with different abilities, and consider the shortcomings and 'weak spots' of each employee. It, in effect, leads to more positive collaboration and teamwork, which 'gets it' and encourages more creativity.

Such leaders see emotions and thoughts as crucial, not to be overlooked, and typically dependent on essential latent concepts, perceptions, and understanding. Tap into each employee's emotional and thinking dimension, and they allow them to keep their eyes open, discuss and repeat concepts as they travel through the company and introduce employees to the best circumstances in which they work.

Always wonder if individual firms don't have coordination or cooperation? The solution may be sought in the manner in which the members and staff who represent their actions treat facts and feelings. The details are viewed with a premium – the asset that acquires information and prestige. On the other hand, emotions are hindered in making rational decisions: they add little meaning and foul the surface.

The problem here is that everybody has emotions. The only inference that is possible is one of handling reality and not controlling feelings: a market in which employees do not know or appreciate each other. It is also not shocking that the individuals who serve in these organizations do not co-operate or collaborate.

Emotionally informed leaders actively affect their own emotions and those of others: Being mindful and respectful of each other's thoughts, and then communicating and arguing with them, is just the start. When emotionally wise leaders realize how they (and others) feel and the result of these emotions, they are consciously manipulating and regulating them so that outcomes for the company are drastically improved.

This aggressive monitoring and regulation make them accessible to their staff, not compassionate and inspiring. They are focused and influenced by their measurable actions-a soothing force on those around them. These thoughts and actions are contagious: positivity produces optimistic outcomes. We improve this constructive guidance and treatment using corrective emotional regulation strategies (such as respiratory guidance) and strategic psychological treatment (such as shifting their mindset from pessimistic to positive in response to particular situations).

The most excellent example of a leader showing correctly that management and control in an organization was the organization itself had a kind and valued reputation. A reputation focused on reliability and consistency in its work that encouraged confidence and rendered orders to consumers faster than they could be handled.

The dilemma was that the corporation needed new technologies. The newer ones were obsolete, extremely unreliable, and in desperate need of replacement. But how do we cope with consumers who have been queued for the coming six months?

The only answer was to ride on the go. The new program was still a first customer: it was just a possibility that had to be handled.

However, the magnitude and seriousness of the issue quickly intensified. The collapse of the introduction of the new program happened at the worst possible moment, not by inadequate preparation, but as a result of a clash with unexpected circumstances. Based on the new program, there could not be more consumers, and their guard was only removed because the introduction was deemed a success.

To conclude a long story, the execution tanked. A team of ten people faced fifty hideous consumers, who all had defective goods, was a complete disastrous disaster.

The team's initial reaction was terror, panic, and despairs. How can this be done without being an epic PR disaster?? The response was fast arriving and presented beautifully by the Managing Director.

By acknowledging that and managing the way the staff talked about it, he started a mantra of 'we are where we are.' Worry and anger didn't add a profit to everyone, especially to all the people concerned so that it wouldn't change the situation. The Managing Director took the team together and focused respectfully on how to manage the situation and then delegated responsibilities and transparency to individuals depending on how they felt and what this clause allowed them to do better.

The outcome was excellent. The consumers were not pleased, but the team's constructive and cooperative attitude in engaging them and moving on options positively contributed to the success of the result. Given their initial complaints, not one customer made any official report, and even the customers were very thankful for their wisdom in coping with the whole case.

A lack of emotional discipline or power rarely brings value to an organization is the moral of the story. Answers like terror, rage, or anxiety spread like wildfire; companies full of emotions will never work correctly. On the other hand, strong positive feelings will inspire people to things they didn't think they could. It's all about finding people who can handle and control this stuff in your company.

Finally, emotionally wise leaders have a profound and positive impact on our lives. They help focus and bind the world around them, bring us closer together, and make us feel part of something extraordinary. They create workplaces full of trust and cooperation, which encourage people to think expanded, take ideas, and move them around to the business where they can grow and thrive. They inspire and engage every one of us, including ourselves, by building on the inner sources of power and energy that gives us meaning in our lives and makes us feel we belong to.

The final questions are: why are these leaders no longer here, and why are companies not doing more to reward, promote, and advertise these people?

Nobody wants to shut off their feelings or ignore their opinions, but companies do seem capable of encouraging and enhancing this behavior.

Chapter 11.

Cultivating Empathy in Children

Emotional intelligence can help you improve your relationships, self-awareness, and sensitivity when dealing with others. It requires lifelong learning, and the sooner you start, the better.

When it comes to children, it's best if you nurture these skills from an early age. Today, everyone – including children – is expected to be good at managing different relationships. This means that to be able to successfully adapt to the constantly changing environment we live and work in, children should start practicing basic principles of emotional intelligence philosophy even before they start school.

Those who learn these skills at an impressionable age will find it much easier to fit into the high-tech, high-speed, and culturally diverse world of the 21st century. By helping children develop empathy and a sense of self, you are preparing them for the workplace of tomorrow.

There are many different ways to do this, but it's easiest if these strategies are gradually incorporated into their daily routines. A lot of this can be done through role-playing and games.

4 Ways to Encourage Emotional Intelligence in Children

Be The Way You Would Like Your Children to Be

Be their role model. Behave, speak, and act the way you expect them to.

Acknowledge Positive and Negative Emotions in Your Child

Learn to recognize different emotions in your children and tell them it's okay to be sad, angry, or hurt. Teach them how to resolve conflicts and encourage them to express love or sadness openly.

Encourage Your Children to Accept and Express Their Emotions

Children should feel free to talk about how they feel and why. But they will only do so if you create an environment in which it feels safe for them to open up. Never punish them for something bad they've told you they've done, for they may learn it doesn't always pay to be honest.

Be Realistic

Don't expect results overnight. This is a lifelong learning process. Emotional intelligence is a sign of emotional maturity, so adjust your expectations to their age.

4 Skills to Cultivate in Children

Empathy

Can your child see and relate to another person's pain or happiness? Do they sometimes cry for others? Do they feel sorry if a friend lost something? Or when they see a dead bird in the park? To teach your children to empathize with others, you have to be a perfect example of how they should behave. Don't try to fake empathy if you don't feel it. Children are much smarter than we give them credit for – if you fake, they will, too.

Expression

Children often express their feelings in very socially unacceptable ways, like by screaming or crying. If you try to stop them, you are effectively preventing them from expressing their feelings – indirectly interfering with their development.

When they scream or cry, all they are doing is venting their emotions. It's believed that if you prevent them from expressing their emotions this way, they will express them in another, perhaps more violent way, like by taking it out on a sibling or the dog, or being destructive.

Listening

Being around children can be very tiring: they ask a million questions, they talk non-stop, and they crave attention all the time. If you are busy, exhausted, or simply not in the mood and ask them to shut up or ignore them, you are sending a very wrong message. To develop into an emotionally intelligent person, a child should be given your full attention whenever he or she needs it.

Problem-Solving

Parents often rush to help their children with whatever problem they may be having. However, this makes them dependent on others to solve their problems. To nurture their emotional intelligence, encourage them to find solutions on their own. They may struggle, they may get angry, or even cry if you refuse to help, but when they manage to get it right, it will boost their confidence and will help them grow into independent and responsible adults.

Emotional Intelligence in Teenagers

A high IQ in a child is no longer what parents worry about most. Today, they are encouraged to pay much more attention to their teenagers' emotional well-being. They do this by helping them develop self-awareness and manage their emotions, as well as by boosting their confidence through regular encouragement and praise.

Teenagers are young adults whose brains are still developing, so signs of strong emotional intelligence are not always consistent. However, the main clue is how well a teenager handles their emotions.

8 Traits of Emotionally Intelligent Teenagers

They Are Interested

Emotionally intelligent teenagers are interested in the world around them. They are curious about life and want to know everything.

They Don't Worry Too Much About Making Mistakes

They accept that making mistakes is a part of life. They don't dwell on past mistakes or hurts, and this is a good sign of resilience and an ability to overcome challenges.

They Have a Positive Mindset

They generally focus on what they are good at, rather than on their weaknesses.

They Control Their Emotions

Emotionally intelligent teenagers understand the power that comes with controlling and managing your emotions. They understand their happiness and success is in their own hands.

They Differentiate Between Various Energies in Their Environment

Emotionally intelligent teenagers recognize those among them who boost or drain their energy levels, as well as those who create negative vibes.

They Embrace Change

They don't fear change – on the contrary. They can easily adapt to a new situation or circumstance.

They Don't Hold on to Grudges

Emotionally intelligent teenagers are generally quick to let go and move on after an incident.

Chapter 12.

Success People vs. Non-Success People

There are many different things that separate successful people and non-successful people and the first thing that separates the two is the fact that successful people are disciplined in a way that non-successful people have not yet achieved. We say not yet because it's still possible for them to do that.

What determines a non-successful person from a successful person is not a matter of trying (per se) or a matter of laziness. This is something that most people don't understand. They think that non-successful people could be lazy or that they just don't try hard enough and that's not true in some cases. Though it is true with others. Non-successful people may not know how to get to where they need to be, but in some cases, it's not a matter of them being lazy. It is just a matter of them not utilizing the knowledge that they have or not having the proper knowledge in the first place. Now on the flip side to this, it is worth mentioning that this is true for some cases. It's just as everyone is different and many different things need to be taking into account here.

Now we will go over the differences between both successful and non-successful people. Non-successful people usually disapprove of change and there forever looking for ways that things can go wrong, so they pass up opportunities to make their lives better. They don't entertain the idea that a little change can improve their situation. They don't see that maybe making a little change could make their lives much better. They also judge people's responses and try to undermine other people.

They ask for other people's opinions, but they're judging those answers and ranking them. This doesn't help them, and it hurts the people around them because, in time, people stop giving their honest opinions because they're not being valued. As their not being valued, why would they take you seriously if you're not going to care about anything they have to say. They avoid gratitude because showing gratitude is considered to be a weakness to them. Many non-successful people can say that they feel that the world owes them something and they deserve everything that they get. This is not true of everyone, but it is true of most who are unsuccessful. Another issue that they tend to have is that they refuse to apologize. Having to say that they are sorry may seem like a failure or a loss to them. Non-successful people can feel like they view life a certain way. Perhaps as a competition where they need to get ahead. If this is how they feel, they can tend to take defeat very badly, which makes them unable to apologize. If they feel that they can't apologize because they believe that they are unable to apologize, they have a negative attitude.

Non-successful people are good at finding fault in absolutely everything you could say to them. You could even say that one favorite pastime of a non-successful person is that they love criticizing. They fail to think of

83

solutions but magnify every problem instead and they don't take the chance to learn.

Instead, they let themselves sink into a place that they shouldn't and get depressed. Depression is a real thing and many people suffer from it, so this is not something that was making light of. We're saying that non-successful people do something that can harm them. As depression is so serious were simply saying that you should avoid drowning in negative emotions because it hurts you so much. They don't look at their mistakes as a chance to learn or improve. Instead, they get disheartened and they tend to give up too soon where they shouldn't.

Successful people on the other hand, possess a strong sense of self-awareness which goes back to emotional intelligence. They are not self-oriented, and they do not work with just their own goals in mind. They possess a sense of ownership and they take responsibility and accountability for their actions. They don't try to cover up their mistakes and they don't let those negative feelings stay with them. Instead, they own up to it and then move on. They understand that you have to forgive yourself before you're able to do this. As such, successful people tend not to make the same mistake twice, which helps in their life and career.

They always try to improve and push themselves to step out of their comfort zone because they know that that's what they have to do to be successful in areas of their lives. They are comfortable taking risks and even if they're not, they know that they're necessary (in healthy ways. Healthy risks). They view their failures with a positive frame of mind because they want to explore their opportunity to grow and advance their career to another level. They also have oriented goals to keep themselves motivated. They set targets and goals for themselves. Both short term and long term and their effectiveness in setting the pace of their work.

Another thing that they are clear and realistic about is where they want to go and they also value time due to this fact. This is very important to successful people. They treat time like it's a precious commodity and they understand that they need to use their time wisely. They use it as effectively as they can, so they don't put things off until tomorrow. They get it done today because they understand that leaving things off until it's no longer beneficial. The distinction between successful people and non-successful people in these examples is quite clearly marked so that you can see just how they're different. It's quite simple to see how they are different and what it is that sets them apart. Other examples of how they're different are that successful people ask questions and they analyze their feelings and emotions.

Successful people don't suppress their emotions. This is something that people get confused about. They believe that emotional intelligence is suppressing your emotions. That's not what it is. It's about managing your emotions healthily. They know how to handle them healthily. They yield great results and are highly efficient, but they're still human at the end of the day. What sets them apart is that they understand that their emotions can be handled healthily. We have said this twice to emphasize the fact that you need to express yourself in a way that isn't going to get you in trouble or fired.

They can regulate and manage their emotions because they know how your emotions influence the way you think and the way you act. They understand what can happen from emotional outbursts and how it can hurt you. They also know how to say no when they have a full plate and successful people know that progress comes from saying yes to priority items but saying no to those that aren't because they don't want to spread themselves too thin. They also understand how to stand up to the inner critics but forgive themselves and move on from it so that it doesn't stay with him.

They also tend to focus on the positive things instead of the negative. If you pay attention to the circumstances of your life you'll find the positive events outnumber the negative events. The problem is that we get sucked into the negative by being around the wrong people. Successful people notice the good things that are around them and they choose to be around the people that add value to their life instead of people that don't. Along with the ability to listen more than they talk, they also never stop learning because they understand that reading and learning and exposing yourself to new things every day is the best way to get some new success and continued success. Non-successful people stop growing because they let their egos dictate the false belief that they know everything, but no one knows everything and there's always something more to learn. When you stop learning new things, you cease to challenge yourself with new ideas and you become stagnant. Successful people also recognize that you should surround yourself with people that are smarter than you.

Another tip that successful people also tend to follow is that they tend not to be distracted by another best thing or other people's opinions. They know their true purpose and true mission in life, and they keep them at the forefront of their minds so that they can set out to accomplish every goal that they have for themselves. They know what they want, and they are trying to get it for themselves.

Successful people are also more self-disciplined because they understand the importance of personal management and self-discipline. All great successes in life are precedented by a long period of focused effort on the most important goals that you have for yourself. Self-discipline is something that you can learn, but unsuccessful people may tend to shy away from it instead of going towards it like successful people do. Understanding the differences between successful people and unsuccessful people is going to help you become better and reach for success in your own life because you'll know where to start. Be sure to utilize these tips in your daily life to become a more self-disciplined and a better habit making person. Having better habits in your life is going to be able to make you achieve things more positively and it will help you begin to find out what you feel is important in your life.

Chapter 13.
Setting Goals

Well, who doesn't want to live his or her best life? The thing that you should focus on is what "best" means to you and how you plan on achieving it. If you have ever watched the Oprah Winfrey show, then you would have heard her talking about the "best life" all the time. However, what is the first step in this process? It is essential that you realize that there is a process and goal setting is just a part of it. For instance, you have put in considerable time and effort for figuring out your ideal goal, but then your attitude towards everything, in general, is negative, achieving your goal would be quite difficult. It isn't just about what we know, but it is also about what we practice.

Keep a simple thing in mind before learning about setting goals: Do not worry for even a minute if your objective seems irrational to others. It doesn't matter. Well, if it doesn't scare you a little, it isn't worth doing. Also, crazy ideas are the ones that can revolutionize the world. Here are certain things that you should keep in mind while setting goals for yourself.

Always Start With the Ideal Situation

Here's your chance to dream. Imagine that you have a blank slate and you get to decide who you can be what you want to do. Don't worry about the obstacles immediately, just start with your dreams. There may be various things that you want to do in your life. Start with the possibilities and then you can move onto the practicality of your idea. Yes, don't worry about the bills, the mortgages, or other burdens while dreaming. Think about the ideal version of "you" and then you will have to think of how you can make it a reality.

Always Write Down Your Goals

When you start writing down your goals, you will start seeing the direction you want to head in, and this makes the process of decision making quite simple. This might sound old school, but writing down your goals is very helpful. People usually like keeping everything in their brain instead of writing it down. When you write something down, it provides a sense of clarity. Once you have written your goal or goals down, you should place that paper in a place where you will see it daily. Place a copy of it in your refrigerator or the mirror. This will act as a reminder and will encourage you to think about your goal. This form of repeated exposure helps in focusing your conscious and subconscious mind on what you want to achieve.

Determine Its Importance

You need to be clear when it comes to setting your goals. Why is the goal essential for you? Is it important because your family wants you to do it or because you want to? Your goals shouldn't be the "should be" ones. Well, there are plenty of things that you "should be" doing according to others and the society that we live in. Instead, think about the things that you want to do. For instance, your goal is to lose weight. Now, why is this important for you? Will you take the necessary steps and make the sacrifices required to attain this goal? We often have to make difficult choices while setting goals. That is a part of the process. So, you will need to prioritize.

The primary question that you should be able to answer is whether you will feel a sense of achievement when you achieve the goal or not. For instance, you might have the goal to become the best business in your niche market. But if you want to stay connected to your child and coach your child's softball team, achieving your business goal might or might not leave you feeling satisfied. Yes, you do have to consider such questions, even if they seem tough. So, sit down and start brainstorming for ideas. Don't worry about what you are writing; just write everything down that pops into your mind. Here are a couple of questions that you can ask yourself for figuring out what matters the most to you.

What would I do if I only have six months left to live? What would I do if I never had to worry about my finances? What would I do if I knew that I would never fail?

Once you have answered these questions, sleep on it for 24 hours. Come back after a day and see how you feel about the things that you have written down. Whatever still makes sense to you should be left as it is and now you have a goal to work towards.

Your Goals Should Add Some Meaning to Your Life

Your goals should never be vague. A vague goal can derail you faster than anything else. If you want to become a better basketball player, exercise frequently, or become a better leader, then your goal needs to be certain. Announce your goal and be honest with yourself about whether it lends a sense of clarity or not. Once your goal is clear, then you need to make sure that it is something that you care about and not what others around you care about. Many goals might seem specific, but they, in fact, are quite vague. For instance, a goal that says make getting in shape doesn't make specific if you want to lower your cholesterol levels, reduce weight, improve your stamina, or run a marathon. Getting in shape is vague. Instead, a goal that says, "I want to lose 15 pounds in 3 months" is a specific goal. Building business is an example of a vague goal along with spending more time with friends. The more uncertain your goal sounds, the more likely it is that you will abandon it. A specific goal will provide you with a sense of purpose.

Prioritize and Pursue Your Goal

It is very likely that you will have plenty of important things in your life. So, make a list of all your goals and then select the three most important goals from that list. These three would make up your tier-one goals: the ones that have the potential of altering your life drastically. They aren't necessarily the goals that will help you in minting money or earn you fame, but they are the goals that will lend some meaning to your life. These goals can be big or small and could be something like changing your profession, completing your college, or paying off your student loans. The only condition is that the goals mentioned in tier-one should be of some significance to you.

Setting a Target Date

This is one of the toughest steps, but you need to do it. Listing down a specific goal is just one step, but that doesn't mean anything if you don't create a deadline for yourself. For instance, a goal that says, "I want to lose 15 pounds" is a specific goal but something that says, "I want to lose 15 pounds within three months" makes your goal seem actionable. It gives you a target to work with. When you don't set a deadline for yourself, it is very likely that you will end up procrastinating. Procrastinating is a fundamental human tendency and, without a target, you wouldn't achieve your target. And not just that, having a target also allows you to measure your progress and adjust the pace at which you are going.

Taking Small Steps

You don't need to do everything at once. Take it slow and steady. Once you have managed to finalize a goal that is not just important to you, but excites you as well, the next step is to start taking small steps that will help you in achieving your goal. Stay away from all the strategies that advocate "all-or-nothing." For instance, you want to start your own business, then a simple step that you can take is registering your domain name or even ordering business cards. One small step a day can help you in achieving excellent results. Achieving your goals is a process and not magic, so it does take a while.

You can create a one-step-a-day rule for yourself. This means that every day you will be doing something, regardless of how small or significant it is, that will help you in achieving your goals. However, give yourself a couple of "off days" as well. There are bound to be some days on which you haven't managed to do anything, or you honestly didn't have the time to do anything. It is okay and don't be too hard on yourself. Every day offers you a new opportunity and go ahead and grab it.

Make a to-Do List

Making a to-do list is quite helpful. Take a sheet of paper and list down all the things that you have to do on that particular day. You can either do this as soon as you wake up in the morning, or you can make your to-do list on the previous night before going to bed. So, when you wake up in the morning, you will have a sense of direction, and you will know what needs to be accomplished by the end of the day. A to-do list also helps in relieving your anxiety about a particular task. A to-do list is convenient, and it will help in making sure that you don't forget anything. For instance, if you have got to spend about three hours attending meetings and have got eight hours of work after that, then it is unlikely that you will be able to get everything done. A to-do list will merely tell you the number of things you will need to get done, but it won't tell you the number of hours you have got for completing these tasks. If you want your to-do list to be of some value, then you will need to make sure that you have allocated your time for different things. When you have assigned your time for various tasks, then you will realize the tasks that are feasible and the ones that aren't. By doing this, you will be able to prioritize your day and get started with the tasks that are a priority and leave the rest for later. Setting goals will not do you any good if you don't monitor your progress. Keep an eye on your performance and see what you have done so far in the day. If you feel that you are lagging behind, then you can tweak your goals in such a way that you will be able to get done with your work.

Chapter 14.

How Intuition Affects Your Decision

Have you observed how much of a cycle our daily living has become? That to some extent, when we have little adventures, or changes in the routine we're used to, we look like penguins lost in a jungle? This kind of daily living will mold you into phases which are the only ones predictable to you, and you will never be able to train yourself to adapt to new paradigms out of your comfort zone. Nonetheless, the more dynamic and less structured our life gets, we become more efficient in decision-making. This is because our intuition gains more and more recognition as an essential decision-making tool. And the more this is practiced, the more effective people are at recognizing the most appropriate or best option to choose. Besides that, experience also gets to teach us how to effectively map out the course of action in many tricky situations.

This is intuition – it's one of the primal skills we had even before civilizations began. We have instinct as much as animals do, but now, most of us don't have much control over it. However, it's still there, 'at the back of our mind,' the subconscious, waiting to be pulled into action when necessary, but most of the time, it offers help that saves us a week of thinking through logical planning. It is sometimes referred to as our heuristics, a very good tool for decision making. But before we power up our intuition, a few points to remember might come in handy.

Does It Break or Make You?

As mentioned, it is primal to us, as natural beings, animals before civilizations. Our ancestors have used this before to survive, just like a lion preying on a stag or that cheetah chasing a helpless llama. It's somehow a reflex, it is always a part of us, whether we use it or not. And while it is a good thing to know it can never be unlearned, just like our skills in math or biking, it also grows weak and rusty if we don't practice it.

First of all, switch from 'seeing is believing' to 'believing is seeing.' Stop being such an empiricist freak who always has to know everything so that you can grasp and control it. Though it is important to practice it, intuition is still a part of our mental process, and it doesn't need grasping, it knows what we know. Also, challenge yourself with a technique. Intuition isn't supposed to need a 'technique,' but since it is almost never used, we have to develop it enough to use it 'as is' for it to be utilized properly.

The simplest way to understand your 'inner voice' is to see it not as a separate entity from your whole mental process. Think of it as an advanced pattern recognition device. Even without your conscious knowledge, your subconscious mind always automatically searches for connections between your new situation and various patterns from your past experiences. You don't have to consciously recall those experiences. It just acts like a reflex – rapidly remembering and projecting lessons learned into new circumstances in the present, and sends you warnings and sometimes, messages of wisdom, without even thinking hard about it. This is why we always say 'I just know it' because there's no way to know how our subconscious mind works unless we are subjected to professional hypnotic processes. Since we can't explain it in specific words, most of the time, it is expressed in the language of our feelings. This draws the line between overthinking and intuition, because the latter doesn't really need conscious 'thinking.' Between the two, intuition is the most efficient in many ways, as overthinking is harmful as always. If you integrate intuition successfully, you'll be surprised how much it changes how you process and choose options.

Is It Really Helpful?

Since intuition lies on your subconscious, it is not a separate entity. Thus, it has no space-time limits, only what's currently happening. It also has no cultural or dogmatic bases, besides your own comprehension and perspective. It contains only all 'relevant' information applicable in your life. During difficult choices and important decisions, intuition is something you can trust, because the information is not coming from other people directly, humans who have a personal interest and lie to you will fail. However, other well-informed humans can manipulate your intuition towards what they want.

Intuition might be very helpful, but it is also important for your consciousness to do its part. It may be helpful most in navigating much faster through unstructured dates. However, even intuition may be misled if too many of your facts are wrong or missing. And yet again, intuition is a part of you, whatever you misunderstand, slightly or entirely, or ambiguously processed problems will certainly mess with your intuition.

It is also most important to listen to your emotions now and again. Strong negative feelings have an enormous effect on your inner voice. If you are stressed or in a bad mood, your intuition may fail through distortion, or it may be overpowered by your strong negative feelings. You may be thinking that strong positive feelings will nurture your inner voice, but those too might overpower your intuition. If you really want to hear your inner voice, get into a state where you aren't having any strong feelings. Be tranquil and let it flow to you, take a walk, or do something refreshing. You may also say your prayers. Forgive and accept. Sigh. Calm your senses. Unclutter your mind.

Finally, integrate elements from the analytical approach to your intuition. In this way, the quality of your intuitive decisions will increase substantially. In particular, try to follow the procedure of the rational analysis first. Organize your thoughts, step by step, make yourself – conscious and subconscious – truly understand what is happening. To some extent, you may write on paper ideas of the main options and the criteria for evaluating choices. Writing down the key facts and factors needed will keep your mind focused, calm, and tidy. Is the same is true for your intuitive, subconscious mind. Through this process, it will penetrate easily and provide choices that are most relevant, realistic and, even without your conscious mind, what you need the most.

In What Ways Does It Break You?

Still, we can't say intuitive decisions are the safest ones. When in fact, it may appear simple, it has its flaws. For one, it may induce enormous consequences on decisions which involve more complex ones such as future revenues, profits, investments, and other business decisions. These are very factual, and possess their critical and technical analysis, which may involve logical analysis. Subjective decisions may be illogical at these particular times.

Most of the time, we don't know if our intuition is wrong until we see the consequence or unless we conduct a scientific experiment eliciting, proving, and validating that it strongly is. One example would be conductors and other judges who use their intuition in choosing orchestra players and even after hundreds of years of this practice, a lot of mishaps still occur.

In fact, we actually have no idea when to trust our intuition in the future, because we only have a retrospective perspective in validating our decisions. It is difficult to depend on things like this, especially when you are controlling the environment through reasons and logic. Distressing feelings in the process of decision making will only distort your interpretation of your inner voice. This will lead to numerous errors you may suffer from in the long run.

Since intuitions are one part of your mind, the thing is that erroneous kinds of intuitions may actually extend to every other domain of cognition. For one, we have the issue of the eyewitness memory.

Examples/Situations

Empiricism such as the scientific world follows, an order or process in proving factual data. Included are the ways in which facts offered as theories are being measured with their reliability. This is done by repetition and re-iteration of the experiments to repeatedly and consistently prove these facts. It is one of the main disadvantages of intuition, in cases of experiments, it is not reproducible.

Consider a high school professor with an extraordinary intelligence and a doctor's degree in several fields. Given that he is capable of answering almost all kinds of questions, and he will respond correctly and sincerely if you ask him these questions. You might want to test to see if the responses of that professor can be repeated exactly all the same. You ask him the same question ten times, and it is likely the second or third time you ask, the professor will not answer anymore or will give you a wrong answer. Thus, we can say that this professor is non-reproducible and that his answers are nonsense or erroneous. This is a perfect example of why scientists don't waste their energy on this topic anymore.

As I mentioned earlier, intuition is something natural. It abides by the laws of nature and is not mechanical. Consider the movements of a programmed cheetah compared with the real one. With certain stimuli, the robot cheetah might be responding in a predictable way, but the real wild one may respond in many surprising ways. In our empirical beliefs, we often mistake nature by turning it into something mechanical. And at some point, we see them as one entity with the exact same characteristics. If you are not fully aware of these natural laws, or more if you do not believe in its existence and prowess, you might make a bad scientific conclusion.

Furthermore, intuition may be too intrusive or 'unpleasant,' to some extent, for those who might receive information that way. It has a strong urge to challenge our 'belief system', it creates conflict to our patterns, offering the threat of our cycle's disruption. Still, it lies, the best way to grow and evolve into a much better entity is to be challenged and destabilized in our beliefs.

Conclusion

Information overload is sometimes the consequence suffered by those people who base their decisions on intuition alone. Not only that, but they also find it hard to follow simple rules in their day to day lives. The intuition is normal, it is fine to have the 'gut feeling' but only for small decisions where the mind may process some part or information one may possess quickly, automatically, and no consciousness on any details. As a working part of your mind, it is fully functional, even without our control, but it doesn't work as accurately as our conscious mind.

However , never underestimate a person who makes his decisions based on his own intuition, for those are the people who feel free and justified. Because they are the ones, who follow their heart. And now, having read this writing, I bet you have enough knowledge to be one of them as well.

Do keep in mind that in making a decision, you have to be able to achieve balance in using your intuition and facts. Making the best decisions will definitely make life worth living, and you will add a personal touch to every decision by trusting your instincts.